I HAVE A DREAM

SCHOLASTIC PRESS

· · NEW YORK · ·

I HAVE A DREAM

DR. MARTIN LUTHER KING, JR.

FOREWORD BY

CORETTA SCOTT KING

PAINTINGS BY FIFTEEN CORETTA SCOTT KING AWARD

AND HONOR BOOK ARTISTS

, , , , ,

ASHLEY BRYAN	GEORGE FORD
CAROLE BYARD	JAN SPIVEY GILCHRIST
WIL CLAY	BRIAN PINKNEY
FLOYD COOPER	JERRY PINKNEY
PAT CUMMINGS	JAMES E. RANSOME
LEO AND DIANE DILLON	TERÉA SHAFFER
TOM FEELINGS	KATHLEEN ATKINS WILSON

FOREWORD , , , ,
CORETTA SCOTT KING

MY HUSBAND, MARTIN LUTHER KING, JR., had a great dream for America. He believed that people of all colors and religions could learn how to live together and treat each other like brothers and sisters. In his dream, the people of America would put an end to hatred, injustice, and violence, and a new spirit of kindness, sharing, and unity would spread across the land. He believed that we could achieve this dream if we would all make a commitment to forgiveness, justice, and love for each other.

In this beautiful book, fifteen artists have provided their creative illustrations to demonstrate the beauty of his dream and the beliefs that motivated his life and leadership. Their artistry blends beautifully with the inspired message that he shared with millions of Americans at the March on Washington on that magical day of August 28, 1963. His vision of peace with justice and love for everyone still inspires and challenges us to create the beloved community. His legacy of courage, determination, and nonviolence still lights the way to the fulfillment of his dream. May God give us the wisdom and strength to carry forward his unfinished work.

Coretta Scott King

THE GREATEST DEMONSTRATION FOR FREEDOM IN THE HISTORY OF OUR NATION

I AM HAPPY TO JOIN WITH YOU TODAY in what will go down in history as the greatest demonstration for freedom in the history of our nation.

IT CAME AS A JOYOUS DAYBREAK TO END THE LONG NIGHT OF THEIR CAPTIVITY

FIVESCORE YEARS AGO, a great American, in whose symbolic shadow we stand today, signed the Emancipation Proclamation. This momentous decree came as a great beacon light of hope to millions of Negro slaves who had been seared in the flames of withering injustice. It came as a joyous daybreak to end the long night of their captivity.

IN EXILE IN HIS OWN LAND

BUT ONE HUNDRED YEARS LATER, the Negro still is not free; one hundred years later, the life of the Negro is still sadly crippled by the manacles of segregation and the chains of discrimination; one hundred years later, the Negro lives on a lonely island of poverty in the midst of a vast ocean of material prosperity; one hundred years later, the Negro is still languished in the corners of American society and finds himself in exile in his own land.

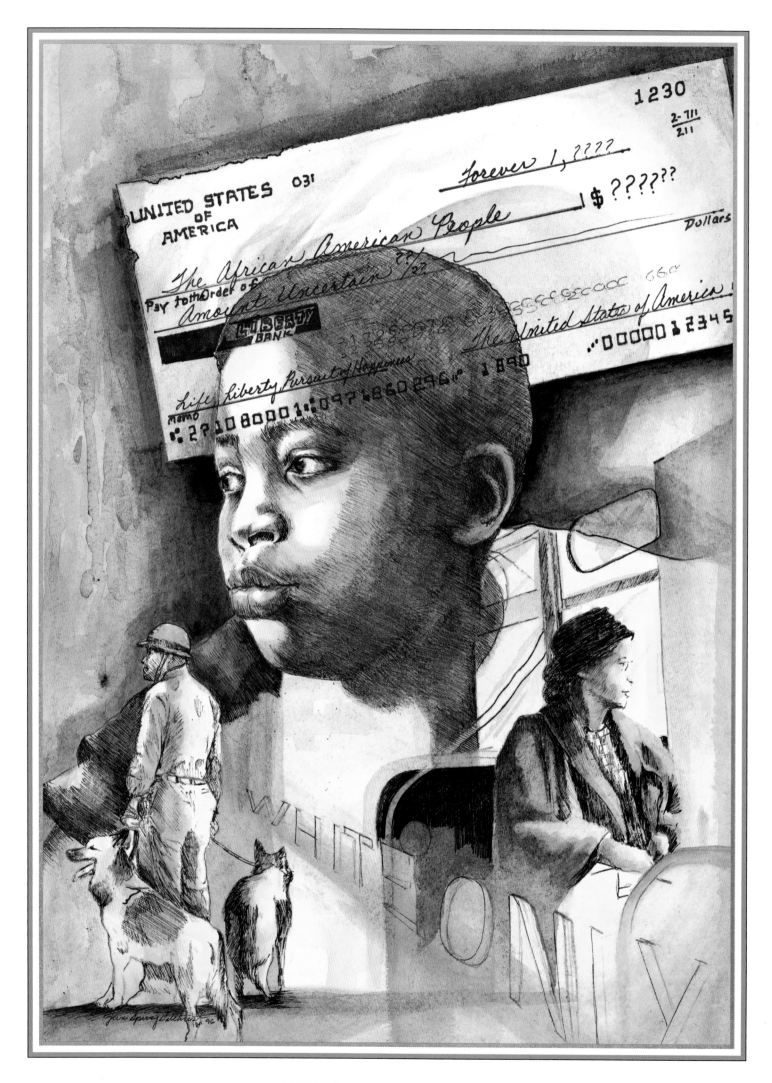

AMERICA HAS DEFAULTED

AND SO WE'VE COME HERE TODAY to dramatize the shameful condition. In a sense we've come to our nation's capital to cash a check. When the architects of our republic wrote the magnificent words of the Constitution and the Declaration of Independence, they were signing a promissory note to which every American was to fall heir. This note was the promise that all men, yes, black men as well as white men, would be guaranteed the unalienable rights of life, liberty, and the pursuit of happiness.

It is obvious today that America has defaulted on the promissory note insofar as her citizens of color are concerned. Instead of honoring this sacred obligation, America has given the Negro people a bad check; a check which has come back marked "insufficient funds." But we refuse to believe that the bank of justice is bankrupt. We refuse to believe that there are insufficient funds in the great vaults of opportunity of this nation. And so we've come to cash this check, a check that will give us upon demand the riches of freedom and the security of justice.

THE SUNLIT PATH OF RACIAL JUSTICE

WE HAVE ALSO COME TO THIS HALLOWED SPOT to remind America of the fierce urgency of now. This is no time to engage in the luxury of cooling off or to take the tranquilizing drug of gradualism. Now is the time to make real the promises of democracy; now is the time to rise from the dark and desolate valley of segregation to the sunlit path of racial justice; now is the time to lift our nation from the quicksands of racial injustice to the solid rock of brotherhood; now is the time to make justice a reality for all of God's children. It would be fatal for the nation to overlook the urgency of this moment. This sweltering summer of the Negro's legitimate discontent will not pass until there is an invigorating autumn of freedom and equality.

THE WHIRLWINDS OF REVOLT

NINETEEN SIXTY-THREE IS NOT AN END, but a beginning. And those who hope that the Negro needed to blow off steam and will now be content, will have a rude awakening if the nation returns to business as usual.

There will be neither rest nor tranquility in America until the Negro is granted his citizenship rights. The whirlwinds of revolt will continue to shake the foundations of our nation until the bright day of justice emerges.

MEETING PHYSICAL FORCE WITH SOUL FORCE

BUT THERE IS SOMETHING THAT I MUST SAY to my people who stand on the warm threshold which leads into the palace of justice. In the process of gaining our rightful place we must not be guilty of wrongful deeds.

Let us not seek to satisfy our thirst for freedom by drinking from the cup of bitterness and hatred. We must forever conduct our struggle on the high plane of dignity and discipline. We must not allow our creative protest to degenerate into physical violence. Again and again we must rise to the majestic heights of meeting physical force with soul force.

The marvelous new militancy which has engulfed the Negro community must not lead us to a distrust of all white people, for many of our white brothers, as evidenced by their presence here today, have come to realize that their destiny is tied up with our destiny and they have come to realize that their freedom is inextricably bound to our freedom. We cannot walk alone.

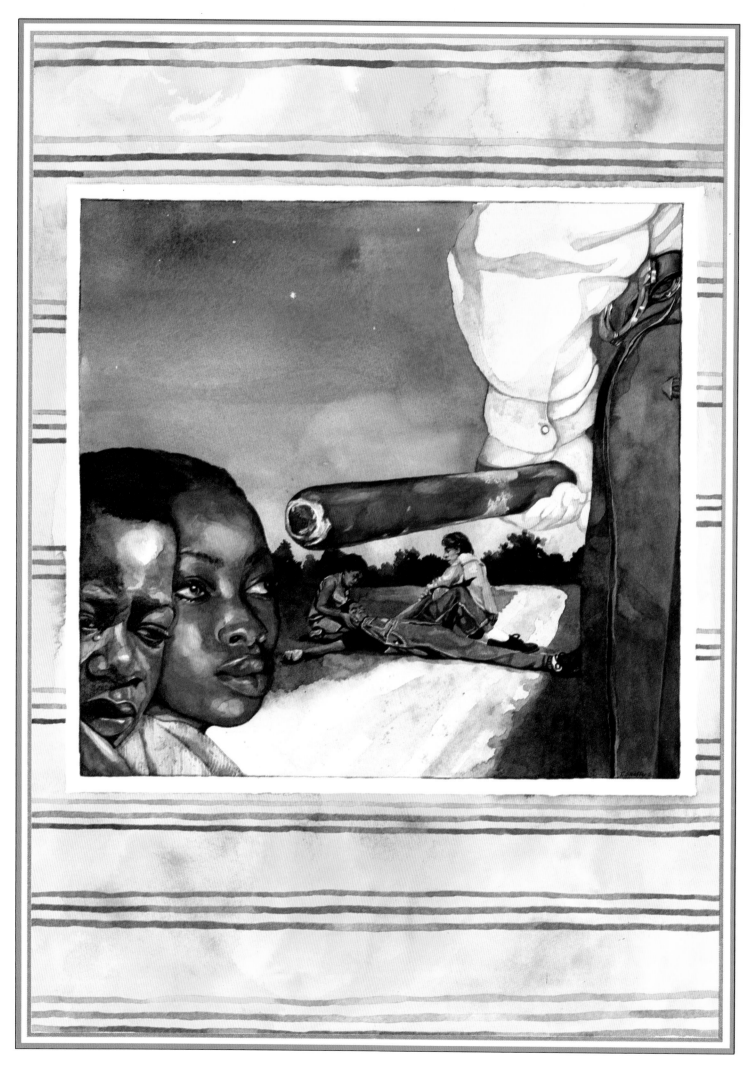

UNSPEAKABLE HORRORS

AND AS WE WALK, we must make the pledge that we shall always march ahead. We cannot turn back. There are those who are asking the devotees of civil rights, "When will you be satisfied?" We can never be satisfied as long as the Negro is the victim of the unspeakable horrors of police brutality.

We can never be satisfied as long as our bodies, heavy with fatigue of travel, cannot gain lodging in the motels of the highways and the hotels of the cities. We cannot be satisfied as long as the Negro's basic mobility is from a smaller ghetto into a larger one.

YOU HAVE BEEN THE VETERANS OF CREATIVE SUFFERING

WE CAN NEVER BE SATISFIED as long as our children are stripped of their selfhood and robbed of their dignity by signs stating, "For Whites Only." We cannot be satisfied as long as a Negro in Mississippi cannot vote and a Negro in New York believes he has nothing for which to vote. No, no, we are not satisfied, and we will not be satisfied until justice rolls down like waters and righteousness like a mighty stream.

I am not unmindful that some of you have come here out of great trials and tribulation. Some of you have come fresh from narrow jail cells. Some of you have come from areas where your quest for freedom left you battered by the storms of persecution and staggered by the winds of police brutality. You have been the veterans of creative suffering. Continue to work with the faith that unearned suffering is redemptive.

Go back to Mississippi; go back to Alabama; go back to South Carolina; go back to Georgia; go back to Louisiana; go back to the slums and ghettos of our northern cities, knowing that somehow this situation can, and will, be changed. Let us not wallow in the valley of despair.

THE TABLE OF BROTHERHOOD

I SAY TO YOU TODAY, my friends, that even though we face the difficulties of today and tomorrow, I still have a dream. It is a dream deeply rooted in the American dream. I have a dream that one day this nation will rise up and live out the true meaning of its creed — we hold these truths to be self-evident, that all men are created equal.

I have a dream that one day on the red hills of Georgia, the sons of former slaves and the sons of former slave owners will be able to sit down together at the table of brotherhood.

I have a dream that one day, even the state of Mississippi, a state sweltering with the heat of injustice, sweltering with the heat of oppression, will be transformed into an oasis of freedom and justice.

I HAVE A DREAM TODAY!

I HAVE A DREAM that my four little children will one day live in a nation where they will not be judged by the color of their skin but by the content of their character. I have a dream today!

I have a dream that one day, down in Alabama, with its vicious racists, with its governor having his lips dripping with the words of interposition and nullification, one day, right there in Alabama, little black boys and little black girls will be able to join hands with little white boys and white girls as sisters and brothers. I have a dream today!

AND THE GLORY OF THE LORD WILL BE REVEALED

I HAVE A DREAM that one day every valley shall be exalted, every hill and mountain shall be made low, the rough places shall be made plain, and the crooked places will be made straight, and the glory of the Lord will be revealed, and all flesh shall see it together.

This is our hope. This is the faith that I go back to the South with.

With this faith we will be able to hew out of the mountain of despair a stone of hope. With this faith we will be able to transform the jangling discords of our nation into a beautiful symphony of brotherhood.

With this faith we will be able to work together, to pray together, to struggle together, to go to jail together, to stand up for freedom together, knowing that we will be free one day. This will be the day when all of God's children will be able to sing with new meaning — "my country 'tis of thee; sweet land of liberty; of thee I sing; land where my fathers died, land of the pilgrim's pride; from every mountainside, let freedom ring" — and if America is to be a great nation, this must become true.

MALINKE ASHANTI QUEEN NEFERTITI FON CONGO DAHOMEY YORUBA
GHANA SUNDIATA FANTI MALI MANSA MUSA MUSLIM IBO SENEGAL BENIN
GOLD COAST TIMBUKTU SONGHAI WOLOF ANGOLA GAMBIA HAUSA NIGERIA
AKAN ELMINA SIERRA LEONE OBEAH RA MENDE AMISTAD SINGBE/CINQUE OLAUDA
EQUIANO BARBADOS GUADELOUPE BRAZIL GORÉE NORTH AMERICA TOUSSAINT
HAITI CUBA JAMAICA MAROONS CUDJOE KOROMANTYN PHILLIS WHEATLEY ZAMBA
NAT TURNER GABRIEL PROSSER DENMARK VESEY HARRIET TUBMAN WILLIAM and
ELLEN CRAFT JOSIAH HENSON HARRIET JACOBS FREDERICK DOUGLASS NUPE
HENRY "BOX" BROWN W. STILL DRED SCOTT MARIE WEEMS W.E.B. DU BOIS LEAR GREEN
HENRY OSSAWA TANNER IRA ALDRIDGE ANNA JULIA COOPER BENJAMIN BANNEK
EDMONIA LEWIS FRANCIS E.W. HARPER WM. WELLS BROWN JAMES P. BECKWOURTH
PRINCE SAU NER TRUTH JAMES WELDON JOHNSON PAUL LAUREN
DUNBAR IDA B. WELLS MARCUS GARVEY CLAUDE McKAY
ZORA NE HURSTON LANGSTON HUGHES CHRISTIAN
MARIANE ON RICHMOND BARTHÉ AUGUSTA SAVAGE CHARLE
DREV PAUL ROBESON GWENDOLYN BROOKS COLTRANE
RALP HT WILMA RUDOLPH CHARLES WHITE A. PHILLIP
RANDO TT TILL ROSA PARKS MARTIN LUTHER KING, JR.
THURGO INE LUCY LOUIS AR STRONG DAISY BATES JAME
MEREDIT HN LEWIS BAKER CHANEY
GOODMA STOKELY RAP BROWN
LORRAINE H KWAME NK HUEY NEWTON
MALCOLM X ELIJAH M NS CYNTHIA
ESLEY DENISE ROBERTSO E. D. NIXON
ESSE JACKSON BAYARD RUS RTHUR ASHE
OTHER HALE N MANDELA PANTHER PARTY
BOB MARLEY NGELA DAVIS TOMMIE SMITH
TEVIE WO MEDGAR EVE JOHN CARLOS
UDRE RIGG MUHAMMAD ALI
JAMES BALDWIN
HN HENRIK CLARKE
BARBARA JORDAN
MARCH ON WASHINGTON
AN MAN MARC

THANK GOD ALMIGHTY, WE ARE FREE AT LAST

SO LET FREEDOM RING from the prodigious hilltops of New Hampshire.

Let freedom ring from the mighty mountains of New York.

Let freedom ring from the heightening Alleghenies of Pennsylvania.

Let freedom ring from the snowcapped Rockies of Colorado.

Let freedom ring from the curvaceous slopes of California.

But not only that.

Let freedom ring from the Stone Mountain of Georgia.

Let freedom ring from Lookout Mountain of Tennessee.

Let freedom ring from every hill and molehill of Mississippi, from every mountainside, let freedom ring.

And when this happens, and when we allow freedom to ring, when we let it ring from every village and every hamlet, from every state and every city, we will be able to speed up that day when all of God's children — black men and white men, Jews and Gentiles, Protestants and Catholics — will be able to join hands and to sing in the words of the old Negro spiritual, "Free at last, free at last; thank God Almighty, we are free at last."

DR. MARTIN LUTHER KING, JR.
1929 - 1968

IN HIS LANDMARK SPEECH at the March on Washington, August 28, 1963, Dr. Martin Luther King, Jr. addressed an interracial crowd of over 250,000 people with these words, "I have a dream that one day this nation will rise up and live out the true meaning of its creed...that all men are created equal." And it was this dream that drove Dr. King throughout his life.

Martin Luther King, Jr. was born on January 15, 1929, in Atlanta, Georgia, to a family active in the Baptist ministry. King was a gifted student who entered Morehouse College in Atlanta when he was only fifteen years old; and, in February of 1948, at only nineteen years of age, he was ordained to the ministry at Ebenezer Baptist Church in Atlanta. After receiving his B.A. in Sociology from Morehouse in 1948, he earned a Bachelor of Divinity degree at Crozer Theological Seminary in Chester, Pennsylvania, where he was valedictorian of his class. At Crozer, King became acquainted with Mohandas Gandhi's philosophy of nonviolent protest. King continued his theological studies at Boston University, earning his Ph.D. in 1955.

While in Boston, King met Coretta Scott, an Alabama native who was studying at the New England Conservatory of Music. They were married in Marion, Alabama, on June 18, 1953. The next decade saw the birth of their four children — and Dr. King's rise to the forefront of the Civil Rights Movement.

Dr. King's involvement in the Civil Rights Movement began during his tenure as pastor of the Dexter Avenue Baptist Church in Montgomery, Alabama. On December 1, 1955, a black woman named Rosa Parks refused to surrender her seat on a public city bus to a white passenger and consequently was arrested for violating the city's segregation law. The Montgomery Improvement Association, with Dr. King as its elected leader, organized a boycott of the city's buses. The boycott lasted for over a year and finally ended successfully in the desegregation of Montgomery's public bus system.

This victory elevated Dr. King's national visibility, introducing him as an eloquent and dynamic leader. On the heels of the success in Montgomery, Dr. King organized the Southern Christian Leadership Conference, which he led until his death in 1968. As president of SCLC, Dr. King toured the country and the world, meeting with prominent civil rights and religious leaders.

In 1960 Dr. King returned to his native Atlanta. During these next years, the height of the Civil Rights Movement, Dr. King had to test his doctrine of nonviolence often, as he was arrested thirty times for his participation in civil rights demonstrations. A protest in Birmingham, Alabama, in the spring of 1963 put Dr. King in prison. There he wrote *Letter from Birmingham Jail*, which expanded his theory of nonviolence. In August 1963, Dr. King joined other civil rights leaders in organizing the historic March on Washington to demand equal justice for all citizens under the law. And by 1964 the efforts of the Civil Rights Movement culminated in the passage of the landmark Civil Rights Act of 1964. In December of 1964, Dr. King was awarded the Nobel Prize for Peace.

Dr. King traveled to Memphis, Tennessee, in 1968 to support a strike by the city's sanitation workers. On April 4, while standing on the balcony of a motel, Dr. King was shot and killed. The assassin, James Earl Ray, pleaded guilty, but later recanted, and without a jury trial, he was sentenced to ninety-nine years in prison.

Dr. Martin Luther King, Jr.'s legacy lives on. The books he wrote, the speeches he delivered, the lives he touched, all have empowered us to fulfill his enlightened dream.

ABOUT THE ARTWORK IN THIS BOOK

All of the artists in this book are recipients of the Coretta Scott King Award and/or have been named Coretta Scott King Honor Book artists for their work in previously published books.

The Coretta Scott King Award is presented annually by the Coretta Scott King Task Force of the American Library Association's Social Responsibilities Round Table. Recipients are African American authors and illustrators whose distinguished books promote an understanding and appreciation of the culture and contribution of all people to the realization of the "American dream." The award commemorates the life and work of Dr. Martin Luther King, Jr. and honors his widow, Coretta Scott King, for her courage and determination in continuing the work for peace and brotherhood.

I HAVE A DREAM · · · LEO AND DIANE DILLON

"In our painting, the light that Dr. King is approaching represents the dream achieved. He is accompanied by the spirits of equality and justice. To keep the dream from fading, we must always keep moving toward it." { JACKET AND FRONTISPIECE ART } SIZE: 16¾ X 16¾ MEDIUM: ACRYLICS

THE GREATEST DEMONSTRATION FOR FREEDOM IN THE HISTORY OF OUR NATION · · FLOYD COOPER

"In my painting, I used color as a metaphor to convey the feeling of the day. It was a day most often remembered in black and white, due to the confines of the medium of the 60s that recorded the event. This afforded me great freedom as I set out to capture the emotions of the speech through color. The many different colors represent the many life experiences that came together to make a single, powerful statement. Even the Washington Monument seemed to be a fist raised for the cause!" SIZE: 20 X 12¾ MEDIUM: OIL WASH ON BOARD

IT CAME AS A JOYOUS DAYBREAK TO END THE LONG NIGHT OF THEIR CAPTIVITY · · · JERRY PINKNEY

"In this painting, I have tried to speak to and celebrate the courage and heroism of the children, women, and men who fought against slavery through resistance — even though many were enslaved themselves.

"The Emancipation Proclamation provided the opportunity for newly freed slaves in the South to take up arms against the forces and institutions that had kept them chained to an unjust and immoral circumstance.

"Now, black children, women, and men could participate in their own destiny."

SIZE: 13⅜ X 17⅛   MEDIUM: PENCIL AND WATERCOLOR ON PAPER

IN EXILE IN HIS OWN LAND · · · PAT CUMMINGS

"Dr. King's words evoke vivid memories of turbulent times. Having lived through those years and having seen, first hand, what impact Dr. King had on all of our lives, his words bring only hopeful images to mind. So, I chose to portray a contemporary man who walks towards a city with confidence and strength, prepared to collect on what is promised on that shining horizon. The shadow that is cast behind the man, however, is the shadow of his past, the shadow which creates whatever shackles still remain. Even so, he continues to move forward with strength, he never breaks his stride."   SIZE: 15 X 18   MEDIUM: OIL OVER ACRYLICS

AMERICA HAS DEFAULTED · · JAN SPIVEY GILCHRIST

"The symbols I used for America's shame and broken promises (check, dogs, and policemen) are contrasted by a symbol for strength, endurance, and perseverance (the elder) and that of pride, innocence, hope, and the future (the child). The struggle continues, but the hope keeps us strong."

SIZE: 9 ¾ X 14¼   MEDIUM: PEN AND ACRYLICS

THE SUNLIT PATH OF RACIAL JUSTICE · ASHLEY BRYAN

"Dr. Martin Luther King, Jr.'s 'dream' of freedom, justice, and equality is every human being's right! In my painting, children are playing together. As every living person is either a child or has grown through childhood, I use this theme as a metaphor to celebrate and embrace all people, all ancestries, all creative and caring human endeavors."

SIZE: 7⅛ x 9⅝   MEDIUM: TEMPERA AND GOUACHE

THE WHIRLWINDS OF REVOLT · · BRIAN PINKNEY

"I chose to illustrate the 'whirlwinds of revolt' by using 'wind' in my art to suggest the collective energy of people coming together for a common goal. This energy is forever pushing the nation toward positive change."   SIZE: 9½ x 10½   MEDIUM: SCRATCHBOARD, LUMA WATERCOLOR, AND GOUACHE

MEETING PHYSICAL FORCE WITH SOUL FORCE · GEORGE FORD

"Imagine the courage of the young civil rights volunteers facing the hate-filled mobs who would deny blacks — and any whites with them — the right even to sit and eat at a public lunch counter.

"Whenever in our struggle for equal justice we feel tempted toward bitterness or hatred, we can gain inspiration and hope by reminding ourselves of the true meaning of Dr. King's words, 'soul force.'

"Meeting physical force with soul force gives us a weapon that cannot be opposed and provides us with the inner strength to endure any suffering until right is triumphant."

SIZE: 10¼ x 13⅝   MEDIUM: PENCIL, ACRYLICS, AND WATERCOLOR

UNSPEAKABLE HORRORS · · · · TERÉA SHAFFER

"This painting depicts the horrors but also the unity that occurred during the Civil Rights Movement. During the movement, many blacks suffered brutal beatings by police. Yet, these were times of crisis when people, black and white, rallied together, found strength together, and came together as one. In this sense Dr. Martin Luther King, Jr.'s dream was, and is, becoming a reality."

SIZE: 13½ x 18   MEDIUM: OIL, WATERCOLOR, GESSO, AND COLOR PENCIL

YOU HAVE BEEN THE VETERANS OF CREATIVE SUFFERING · · · · · · · TOM FEELINGS

"Throughout the centuries, Africa's powerful celebratory rites have always acted as a spiritually strong balancing force to counter the painful experience of slavery. Clearly evident in black music, black dance, and the world of athletics, wherever there is a level playing field, we innovate, we improvise within that restrictive form, then transcend it, raising the level of excellence. In the words of writer Paule Marshall, 'we are a people who transformed humiliating experiences into creative ones.'"   SIZE: 8 X 10½   MEDIUM: LINE ETCHING PRINT / CHARCOAL AND PENCIL

THE TABLE OF BROTHERHOOD · JAMES E. RANSOME

"Since childhood, the 'I Have a Dream' speech has both motivated and inspired me. Yet, as an adult, I have developed an even deeper appreciation for the lyrical language and vision of hope it provides, in spite of the harsh realities it discusses. This particular portion of the speech has always been one of my favorites because it seems to reflect the pivotal moment where King's dreams for the future are articulated. The idea of former slaves and slave owners coming together for the sole purpose of enjoying each other's company is a tribute to the depth of human spirit and compassion."

SIZE: 18½ X 24½   MEDIUM: OIL ON PAPER

I HAVE A DREAM TODAY! · · · · · WIL CLAY

"My painting illustrates the joy and excitement I often share with children of different backgrounds who perform for me when I visit schools around the country. It is quite an inspiration: the dream lives on today.

"While there has been much progress towards achieving Dr. King's far-reaching ideals for our nation, our struggle must continue. Each generation to hear Dr. King's hopeful words should be duty-bound to apprise each new generation of its value and importance to our future."

SIZE: 30 X 40   MEDIUM: ACRYLICS

AND THE GLORY OF THE LORD WILL BE REVEALED
, , , , , KATHLEEN ATKINS WILSON

"In his 'I Have a Dream' speech, Dr. Martin Luther King, Jr. selected the comforting biblical prophecy from Isaiah 40:4, 'and the glory of the Lord shall be revealed,' to remind us of His power over all circumstances. I chose to intrepret Dr. King's words through a magnificent landscape to symbolize a place where God reveals Himself; where peace, and freedom, and beauty prevail; where our faith is renewed and our hopes and dreams are kept alive."

SIZE: 18 X 24   MEDIUM: MIXED-MEDIA WATERCOLOR

Kathleen A. Wilson

THANK GOD ALMIGHTY, WE ARE FREE AT LAST
, , , , , , , , CAROLE BYARD

"As I read these words of Dr. Martin Luther King, Jr., somewhere in the middle, my blood is rushing. I am out of my seat, I walk the room, moving my hands, raising my voice, swaying to the rhythm. I see the past, I remember where we came from, who we were, who came before, how we got here. I remember the loss, the work, the strength, the determination, the work, the building of a nation, the work, the horror, the love, the prayers, the risks, the chances, the getting by, the standing up, the narrow escapes, the bravery, the star, the song, the light of those who paved the way, the light of our future.

"In my painting is a wall of names, names that came to me as I began to feel my way into the page. They are names of countries, tribes, languages, people, herbs — a heritage of resistance and forging ahead — whatever it took to bring us through."   SIZE: 24 X 15¼   MEDIUM: ACRYLICS

Carole Byard

Text copyright © 1963 by Martin Luther King, Jr., copyright renewed 1991 by Coretta Scott King ‣ Reprinted by arrangement with The Heirs to the Estate of Martin Luther King, Jr., c/o Writers House Inc. as agent for the proprietor ‣ Jacket and frontispiece illustration copyright © 1997 by Leo and Diane Dillon ‣ Illustration for pages 6-7 copyright © 1997 by Floyd Cooper ‣ Illustration for page 8 copyright © 1997 by Jerry Pinkney ‣ Illustration for page 10 copyright © 1997 by Pat Cummings ‣ Illustration for page 12 copyright © 1997 by Jan Spivey Gilchrist ‣ Illustration for page 14 copyright © 1997 by Ashley Bryan ‣ Illustration for page 16 copyright © 1997 by Brian Pinkney ‣ Illustration for page 18 copyright © 1997 by George Ford ‣ Illustration for page 20 copyright © 1997 by Teréa Shaffer ‣ Illustration for page 22 copyright © 1997 by Tom Feelings ‣ Illustration for page 24 copyright © 1997 by James E. Ransome ‣ Illustration for page 26 copyright © 1997 by Wil Clay ‣ Illustration for page 28 copyright © 1997 by Kathleen Atkins Wilson ‣ Illustration for pages 30-31 copyright © 1997 by Carole Byard ‣ Photograph for page 32 copyright © 1964 by Flip Schulke

LIBRARY OF CONGRESS CATALOGING-IN-PUBLICATION DATA

King, Martin Luther, Jr., 1929-1968 ‣ I have a dream / Martin Luther King, Jr. ; illustrated by 15 Coretta Scott King Award and Honor Book artists. ‣ p.   cm.   ‣ ISBN 0-590-20516-1 ‣ 1. Afro-Americans—Civil rights. ‣ 2. Civil rights movements—United States History—20th century. ‣ 3. United States—Race relations. ‣ I. Title. ‣ E185.61.K53 1997 ‣ 305.896'073—dc20 95-45189 ‣ CIP

The estate of Dr. Martin Luther King, Jr. is managed by Intellectual Properties Management Inc., Atlanta, Georgia.

The text type is set in Monotype Dante ‣ Book design by David Saylor

2   4   6   8   10   9   7   5   3

Printed in the United States of America   37

FIRST EDITION, NOVEMBER 1997